FAITH THAT ENDURES

FAITH THAT ENDURES

A STORY OF HOPE AND PERSEVERANCE

JOEL STOCKSTILL

Printed in the United States of America
10 9 8 7 6 5 4 3 2 1

ISBN 978-0-9890909-0-2

Editing by Edit Resource, LLC
Eric Stanford
eric@editresource.com

Copyediting by Brenda Pitts
www.brendapittseditorial.com

Cover design by Dustin West & Bethany Church

Interior design by Silver Feather Design
Yara Abuata
www.silverfeatherdesign.com

Design Directors:
Amie Stockstill and Laura Hawkes

To the loving memory of my first wife,
Amy Hart Stockstill

Amy, your inspiration lives on in our hearts.
You are truly "the mother of millions."

contents

foreword ix

preface xiii

chapter one 1

THE FIGHT OF FAITH
*An unexpected diagnosis sets off an extended battle
for my health and my trust in God*

chapter two 13

A MIRACLE OF FAITH
*When medical science fails me, the miraculous
power of God comes through*

chapter three 31

THE REVELATION OF FAITH
*I come to understand how I am joining Jesus in the
fellowship of His suffering*

chapter four 49

THE CALL OF FAITH
*In the midst of my own health trouble, God lays a
burden for the next generation on my heart*

chapter five _____ 63

    THE LIFE OF FAITH

    God sends me a loving partner for my work and
    trials

chapter six _____ 79

    THE TEST OF FAITH

    I give my wife back to God, learning to trust in Him
    even in the worst of circumstances

chapter seven _____ 95

    THE ENDURANCE OF FAITH

    God restores the sparkle to my eye: a new beginning

conclusion _____ 113

foreword

It is a great joy to be able to write a foreword for one of your sons. It is a testimony that the next generation has come of age and is beginning to speak and shape our world with their own callings.

Joel is my firstborn. From his childhood, he memorized Scripture and told Bible stories with passion. That passion only grew through the years as he moved into manhood.

His life changed dramatically at sixteen when his kidneys failed and he started dialysis. It was at that time God's call upon His life became crystal clear and he submitted to it. By nineteen, he was preaching at our large church in Baton Rouge. His subsequent marriage to

Amy Hart triggered one of the greatest moves of God among youth in our nation as up to seven thousand youth gathered weekly in small groups.

Amy's untimely death from cancer again threatened Joel's future. Again he rose up in the strength of God and continued forward. His second wife, Amie, a product of our youth ministry, was joined to his side, and the powerful Bethany internship program developed.

Perhaps you have never walked through what Joel has been through in his thirty-four short years on earth. His message to you, however, regardless of what you are facing, is *hope*.

Hope has kept Joel moving forward into his future against all odds. His powerful podcasts, blogs, and now television programs are inspiring an entire new generation of American believers. His schedule in the near future is almost totally full in spite of the hindrance of dialysis.

If Joel can make it, you can make it too! Grab on to the rich truths of this book that have been forged in the fires of tribulation. Let those truths transform you into a powerful, tempered disciple of Jesus Christ. Then multiply those truths into others that you choose to disciple. That is Joel's vision, and that was Christ's method.

Your life will never be the same after reading this short book. Your future is before you, and Joel's example can encourage you. As my father has said to all of us many times, "Your best is yet to come!"

—LARRY STOCKSTILL

preface

Have you ever been through a trial of your faith? Have you ever wondered if God cares about your situation? Has it ever seemed as if the fulfillment of a promise of God would never come?

Questions like these have challenged believers since it all began with Abraham. So many believers have had these questions and yet felt unable to express them for fear of saying something wrong or being rejected.

I understand.

I am a pastor's son. A youth pastor trying to reach a generation with the gospel. A long-embattled kidney patient. A widowed and re-married husband.

This book is the story of my life—a story that now spans two decades of amazing miracles and devastating hardships. It is not a rags-to-riches story that leaves you with a happily-ever-after feeling. But in a day when everything seems like it's supposed to be fast and easy, this story will challenge you to endure in your faith no matter how hard things get or how long they go on.

I pray your heart will be encouraged as this testimony of endurance unfolds before your eyes with transparency and the ultimate tone of victory in Christ.

chapter one

THE FIGHT OF FAITH

An unexpected diagnosis sets off an extended battle for my health and my trust in God

"These are the times when we must face the giants of our promised land with the fight of Caleb and Joshua inside us and a confidence of the Lord of Hosts guiding us."

One hot Louisiana day in July 1995, when I was sixteen years old, I sat in a doctor's office with my parents on either side of me as my nephrologist (kidney specialist) outlined what lay ahead for me. I began to hear things about my immediate future that scared me to the point of nausea.

But before I get to what I heard, let me back up briefly to tell you how I'd arrived at this day.

Four years earlier, in October 1991, I had been diagnosed with kidney problems through some swelling in my ankles. The doctors didn't know what had started this kidney issue, but they told me that it would most likely not be a big deal until much later in life. This was definitely good news because my life up to this point had been somewhere between average and perfect. Yeah, I had to get some Coke-bottle glasses at seven and braces at twelve, but other than a tonsillectomy and the chickenpox, I had been as healthy as a horse. Blessed to be raised in the godly home of Larry and Melanie Stockstill, the pastors of a church called

Bethany World Prayer Center that I thought was better than Disneyland, I was expecting a wonderful and relatively easy life.

Back to the uncomfortable seat in the doctor's office.

My nephrologist told my parents and me a couple of facts. First, my kidneys were failing fast. That fact was shocking, but the second was beyond comprehension: I would be placed on kidney dialysis while I awaited a kidney transplant. I couldn't believe it! Getting a transplant seemed like an idea from a sci-fi thriller.

After the doctor appointment, my parents took me to one of my favorite restaurants so I could eat a good meal and get a little distance from that surreal appointment. Instead of accepting the truth, though, I began to drift into serious delusion and false comfort, telling myself that life was going to stay pretty much the same for me, that all those horrible things I had just heard were an overreaction. After all, years earlier I had been told that my problem was going to be minor till I was much older. And I was *not* older!

At the age of sixteen, my life was all about using my newly acquired driver's license, playing basketball every day, and chasing cheerleaders around the gym. Could it really be that things were about to become different forever? Was the life I had lived, and had foreseen continuing into my future, really going to be decimated by some strange coincidence of illness?

I wasn't ready to accept it. But these changes were really happening.

And a new life of faith was waiting to begin.

The Fight Inside

When people receive a bad report from a doctor, or a call from their financial advisor saying that all is lost, or an eerie ring in the night heralding the news that a loved one has passed or has been in a tragic accident, the story of faith begins. When things are bumping along just fine and all is well from our perspective, the faith that we are forced to call on isn't much, if indeed it's anything at all.

In a day when people think they are doing Jesus a favor by attending His house once a month, there has been a drastic erosion of what it means to have great faith and for that great faith to be tested and built. In the parable of the sower, the enemy comes and scoops up the seed immediately, and some who have received the seed of the Word never have a chance to grow precious fruit for the kingdom (Mark 4:15). Likewise, the enemy will try to rock your faith with circumstances and trials that don't fit within the parameters of your expectation. If you're like most people, you don't expect negative things to happen to you. But the reality is that sooner or later something is going to knock you off the pedestal of normal and plunge you into the "opportunity" of great defeat or supernatural victory. And what are you going to do then?

Paul's statement to the Philippians—"I can do everything through Christ, who gives me strength" (Philippians 4:13)—is meant to be more than a pep talk for a junior high algebra test. Somewhere in the midst of a devastating blow or a rising tide of adversity in your life, there has to be something that stands up and fights for the victory of Calvary in your situation. That fight is the fight of faith.

I tell many people that in the early years of my struggle with illness, I did not have a deep, abiding faith that rested on the pillar of God's Word. My parents did, and I thank God for their daily and sometimes hourly prayers that helped sustain me. But for me, it was a deep sense of fight within that carried me through the unspeakable circumstances that followed that awful day in the doctor's office.

Did everything the doctor say come to pass? Yes! And even more!

Was it the end of the world? No. But it sure felt like it!

There are times when the Lord will extend His rescuing hand and deliver us swiftly from the hand of the enemy. But then there are *other* times. Oh, those other times!

It's like in Hebrews 11. After a long catalog of people who triumphed through faith, verse 35 says, "But others..." And then the chapter goes on to refer to people who suffered and died in terrible ways. Sometimes *we* are those "others."

Sometimes the Lord allows our faith to be tested. These are the times when we have to recognize the fight before us. These are the times when we must face the giants of our promised land with the fight of Caleb and Joshua inside us and a confidence in the commander of the Lord of Hosts guiding us (Numbers 14:6–9; Joshua 5:13–15).

Starting on August 25, 1995, I was placed on hemodialysis three times a week for up to four hours at a time. The clinic I was sent to had no patients under the age of sixty-five except for me, and many of my fellow patients were missing a limb after a long battle with diabetes. I had landed in another world! It might as well have been the moon. My life was suddenly rocked beyond recognition, and what had been a minor issue was now an all-consuming trauma.

Like a volcano that goes from inactive with occasional smoke to a full-fledged eruption that can be felt for thousands of miles, my life was exploding. Like a boat, I was in a rapid of sorts that would carry me miles down the river of adversity. Like a student, I was being tutored in the art of suffering. Over the next three years, I would endure things that would never enter the wildest imagination of a healthy person, and I would go through it all in an attempt to live. The fight in me drove me to press on.

Know Your Enemy

If you're facing a situation of grave proportions, let me clearly state to you that if you lie down and try to ignore or deny the battle at hand, you will be defeated. You must arrive at a sense of acceptance that the trial you are in is real. You must come to a point where it dawns on you that there is a real enemy out there who goes around "like a roaring lion, looking for someone to devour" (1 Peter 5:8) and that, if given the chance, he will "steal and kill and destroy" everything in your life (John 10:10).

Jesus said that if a strong man knew that an enemy was coming, he would guard his house and be ready (Luke 11:21). Satan is that strong man, and he wants to hold on to every bit of territory he possesses in your life. Only a stronger man—Jesus—can dislodge him. We're victorious against Satan only as we fight in the strength of the Lord.

Maybe today as you read this book, all is well with you, and the battle has not yet come to your door. If so, then you must be ready for it, arming yourself with a true faith resting on God's Word.

Maybe you're in the beginning, middle, or extended season of a trial. Maybe your hope has waned and your faith grown weary. If so, you must make a fresh decision today that something is going to change. That "something" is to embrace the fight of faith. It is to decide that you will no longer fight with carnal weapons, but that you will fight with mighty weapons given to us for the pulling down of strongholds (2 Corinthians 10:4).

I can tell you right now by the Spirit of God that what you are facing is the result of a demonic strong man who has come into your house illegally (or even legally, if you have allowed sin and compromise to enter your life) and whom you must cast out in the Lord's name. You cannot win the battle against this strong man with your mind, your emotions, or even your will. You will win the battle only through fighting the fight of faith with weapons like obedience, surrender, and brokenness.

This is a lesson I learned slowly over time. Little did I understand when I started dialysis that my trials with health, and my challenges of faith, had only just begun.

Fiery Trials
July 27, 2012

A POEM FOR JONATHAN

Fiery trials will inevitably descend
The question being not if but when
Its mask will not be one of great plan
But its presence will grind like mortar and sand

For every great leader its presence has felt
Causing many times your courage to melt
While other moments feeling beat by a belt

The sting of defeat
The loss of a loved one
The unending pain of constant retreat
The gnawing voice that screams you're done

Fiery trials have not come of late
When they began, we're not sure of a date
One thing we know for blessed sure
They somehow cause our faith to be pure

The focus of issues that cannot be beat
Their torment faster than any move of the feet
When dodging and ducking would normally work
The pursuit of this foe you're never to shirk

When will there be a solution? you say
But the fiery trial doesn't work this way
To bear the suffering is real anyway
But to fight against will just rub the wrong way

Having heard much of fiery's loud bell
Has made me more than ready to tell
Of too many times it visited my door
With wares of great misery to sell

Take a note from the song of the great lament
Oh, how I wish this season would end!
From where was this fiery trial sent?
Weaving body and soul in its twisted blend

The depth of hell has forged this great tool
Yet God in His wisdom has decided to use
To be bitter would only be fit for a fool
The wise will decide to use it as fuel

As we endeavor the path of this present life
There's no way to opt out of the path that it lights
The fiery sting of its seasonal strife
Onward we move toward next fiery fights

On celestial shores one day we will rest
Never to feel the wrath of its sting
Our lot will fall to the Lord that is best
And forever to worship the Lamb we will sing
Endured to the end from its terrible test

chapter two

A MIRACLE OF FAITH

When medical science fails me, the miraculous power of God comes through

"It is His business to fulfill our faith. It is His timing that matters. Our plans and schemes mean nothing before a mighty God. He is the divine healer and miracle worker."

By January 1999, three and a half years had passed from the time I learned that my kidneys were failing and I was going to have to have a transplant. Three and a half years of regular dialysis to mechanically clean my blood in a way that my kidneys no longer could. Three and a half years of serious turbulence and unbelievable lows in my young life. Yet I battled my way through it all and remained alive and kickin'!

Forced to drop out of high school in the tenth grade because of my health, I had received homeschooling from my loving mother and had eventually gotten my GED on schedule with my fellow high school graduates. Then I made my way to Oral Roberts University in Tulsa, Oklahoma, for a freshman year filled with adventures and more battles with my health. And that's where I was, at age nineteen, in January 1999.

My journey of faith resumed with the next milestone in my life. The seeming sci-fi idea of having another person's organ placed in my body was about to become an actuality.

A Long Way from Normal

After I had been turned down by several transplant sites, the Mayo Clinic in Rochester, Minnesota, finally said they would make me a candidate for a kidney transplant. But I would have to wait for a suitable organ. We didn't know how long that would take.

Then, on January 8, 1999, a call came through our front office at the church from someone who had been a member of our church in years past. The message quickly made its way to my parents' attention, and my father returned the curious call. The man on the other end was a husband who had just lost his wife in an auto accident in which she had fallen out of the back of a truck and had struck her head on the pavement, dying instantly. He painfully recounted the story of what had happened and said he had heard of my situation and wanted to know if he could donate one of his wife's kidneys to me.

This news was both exciting and scary all at the same time! This man whom I had never met was offering me the gift of new life and hope. (I never did have the opportunity to meet this gentleman and wonder to this day what became of him.) Of course, there were matching issues that had to be resolved, but after some examination, there seemed to be a measure of compatibility.

This being established, my mother and I left our Louisiana home (where I was now living, having left ORU because of major health complications) and boarded a plane for snowy Minnesota early the next morning. Three flights later, we were standing in the snow at the tiny Rochester airport trying to fathom the nineteen-degrees-below-zero weather of the North. Once again my life journey had taken me somewhere I would have never thought I'd be or wanted to be!

The next morning, I was wheeled into the operating room. Before sedating me, the surgeon asked if I'd like to see the kidney about to be placed in my body. Of course, being the curious nineteen-year-old that I was, I said yes, and in his hand he held an organ that could change my life back to normal and make this whole nightmare go away—or anyway, so I hoped!

As it turned out, although the operation was a success, the kidney was very weak and took several weeks to begin functioning at a level good enough for me to stop doing dialysis. In the meantime, after I'd left the hospital within a week and was recovering well from the surgery itself, doctors discovered an air hole in one of the connecting urethras, requiring emergency surgery to repair it. The surgeon reopened the original site and fixed the problem. But this time recovery was a whole different story.

Three months later, after many days spent in ICU (with King Hussein of Jordan in the next room protected by bodyguards with turbans on their heads and AK-47s in their hands), I was moved to another room for less critical care. Eventually I was released to a local medical housing lodge for extended-stay transplant patients and then finally released to make my way back home. Looking back, it amazes me to this day that I was able to somehow live through the three months of hell that had transpired since that January day when we'd gotten the call about the available kidney. So many obstacles had stood in my way, yet I had survived and made my way back to the humid bayous of Louisiana.

Weakened to the point of being unable to walk, I remained on the couch at my parents' house from April to August of that year, just trying to live one day at a time and somehow regain enough strength to reenter society. Oh, the desire for things to just be normal! It's amazing how we all dream of grandeur and the fantastic—until we lose the ground of plain ol' normal. And then how we long for the precious familiarity of life, where nothing really happens and you can relish it!

Return to My Call

That summer, in the midst of all that was taking place with my health, the Spirit of God began to visit me about the calling on my life.

At sixteen, in the month preceding my placement on dialysis, I had knelt with my father next to his bed and surrendered my life to the call of God to preach the gospel. After that, I had been in survival mode for the next three years. But now the stirring of the Spirit began to operate inside me, and although I was too weak to do much of anything, I had a strong desire to do whatever the Lord had for me.

Out of the pain and misery of my youth came a cry to be used by the Lord. Out of the desperation of my situation came a holy hunger for more of Jesus and for a chance to bring that Jesus to what I now knew to be a seriously hurting world. No longer the naive sixteen-year-old who lived in a sheltered bubble of normalcy, I was now a man of seasoned battle, and almighty God was tugging strongly at my life.

Over time I would answer that call and begin the process of learning the things of God and the ways of His Spirit. For the first time in my life, the Word of God began to be more than just a perceived "out card" from misery and started being life to my spirit and soul. I remember days when I would lie in the presence of God for six hours while praying in the Spirit and napping for short periods. Still being extremely weak for the majority of the time, and not reaping much benefit from the transplanted kidney, I found great comfort and peace in the presence of the Lord. The CD *The Master's Healing Touch* was my daily soundtrack to soaring into the realms of God's Spirit. Though my body was weak on the outside, my spirit man was rising on the inside!

I like to say that *saturation is the key to sensitivity*. What I mean is that spending hours and hours in God's presence will cause your ears to be tuned to His voice. Like Samson grinding at the wheel every day as his hair grew back, I was spending time at the wheel of affliction while my spiritual strength was growing daily. Oh, how I longed for freedom from my physical pain! But oh, how I loved those times in the presence of the Lord Jesus! Nothing and no one could stop me from bathing daily in the warmth of His soothing presence. Those times were precious and miraculous. They were times of growth and maturing. Inside my broken body, a mighty force of spiritual capacity was being nurtured.

The climax of this season came in 2001 when, at the age of twenty-two, my body could no longer go on.

Miracle in Tulsa

In November 2000, my transplanted kidney, having become diseased with the original problem that had shut my own kidneys down, failed completely. Eighteen months of freedom from dialysis had never been what it was advertised to be, and now I was placed back on dialysis for what would seem to be an eternity beyond what I had ever dreamed.

My primary doctor called me in and explained to my mother and me that I had six months to live *if* I stayed in the bed, or six weeks to three months if I continued to move around and try to minister in the way that I had been. I weighed only 127 pounds even though I was six feet five inches tall, and my fine strands of blond hair were almost completely gone. It seemed as if the end was drawing near for me.

How would the incredible things I had seen from the Lord about my life ever take place if this was really the end?

Had I walked through all this just to become another statistic of illness?

What about the divine stirring in my heart to preach the everlasting good news?

Surely this could not be it!

At one point, despite the strong warning of impending death from my kidney doctors and the possibility of another transplant out of the question, I told the doctor that his grim prediction would be proven wrong and that I was going to live a long life. Boy, *was* he wrong! And yes, I was right!

By faith I was declaring those things that were not as though they were (see Romans

4:17). Like David, I had faced down many lions and bears of sickness and disease, and now this Goliath of death was not about to take me out of this world. I had souls to win. I had messages to preach. I had books to write. I had a family to enjoy. The name of Joel Stockstill was not yet ready for engraving on a tombstone. No, the name Joel Stockstill was yet to resound in the manner of life and legacy to come!

Six months later I was in prayer, and the Lord spoke to me, saying that evangelist Benny Hinn would lay his hands on me and I would be healed. Several weeks after that, I was having supper with my parents when my father mentioned that he was thinking of flying to Tulsa, Oklahoma, to be in the International Charismatic Bible Ministries conference put on by Oral Roberts Ministries. My spirit immediately leapt within me, as I knew from watching Benny Hinn's show that he would be there as a main speaker. I then boldly informed my father that I was going to travel with him and that Benny Hinn was going to lay his hands on me and I *would* be healed. There was no choice about it in my tone, and immediately Dad agreed to take me with him.

Predictably, the trip was difficult for me. But I didn't care one bit, because my faith was being released for divine healing. I had been in a myriad of healing services and been prayed for by many people. But this was going to be different!

After a sleepless night and much suffering of body, I dressed and made my way to the famous Mabee Center on the campus of Oral Roberts University. When we got inside, we were directed to sit about halfway up in the arena. If I had not been on a mission of faith, this would have been fine, but I was bound and determined to be prayed for, and the farther away from the platform I was, the less chance I had to receive prayer. So I headed down to the front to see if I could find anyone I knew from my college days at ORU who could help me. (I had been at the university twice, a year apart, at this point.) And sure enough, I spotted a security guard who was overseeing the seating up front. He recognized me and realized that we had been given poor seats, and like an angel from the Lord, he directed me to the second row on the end closest to the platform. I waved my hand and signaled my father to our newfound seats, knowing that this was a confirmation of God's hand on this day.

As the service went on for three hours, I was drowning in weariness. I fell asleep many times and was almost delirious, but nevertheless, there was something inside me that was determined to stay and receive. This was my faith! I didn't want to go back to the room and lie down. I had lain down and rested enough for a lifetime, and now was my moment to receive something supernatural from the Lord.

As the service came to an end, Benny Hinn stated that he was not going to be praying for anyone individually that day, but that he would pray a corporate prayer over the pastors and leaders. In my head there was a sense of frantic disappointment, but in my heart I knew that God was going to do something great. When the call for prayer was given, I rushed to the front of the platform and was positioned right next to the pulpit. As the man of God prayed over all the pastors, he kept looking at me in a strange way, and I knew God was speaking to him. (Thank God for sensitive men and women of God who know His voice and are willing to obey!) After the corporate prayer was almost over, he stopped and pointed at me, and in his dramatic voice, he said, "Young man, come up here."

I moved like a cat pouncing on its prey. My physical limitations went out the window, and I quickly made my way onto the platform. Pastor Benny would go on to say that the Lord had been dealing with him the whole service about me (despite my sleeping during his message!). He proceeded to prophesy over my life and give me a passage of Scripture from Psalm 89:20–24. This being done, he laid his hands on me—and I went flying back at least ten feet! The power of God had hit me like I had never experienced before.

From that moment in mid-2001, my health began to improve. My hair thickened; I began to gain weight (not much, but thank God, some); and the strength to preach the gospel began to flood my broken physical body. As you will see in the next chapter, this miracle of healing was the transforming moment in launching me into the ministry versus being laid to rest in a coffin. Jesus Christ of Nazareth had touched my body, and even though I was still doing treatments three times a week, I felt a tangible energy and touch of the Holy Spirit upon my life. What had seemed like the darkest of moments in my health and life had now become a shining witness of God's power.

It is His business to fulfill our faith. It is His timing that matters. Our plans and schemes mean nothing before a mighty God. He is the divine healer and miracle worker.

Trust in Him today! Whatever you are facing or have gone through that doesn't make sense to your natural mind, decide today in your spirit that you will trust the Creator, for He has you in the palm of His hand and loves you with an everlasting love (Jeremiah 31:3).

Praise Jesus for the miracle of faith!

The Great Stumbling Block
November 3, 2012

There it stands, so rugged and sure
The object of many lived through the ages
The ancient, mysterious cure
Against the battle of sin that rages

Could it be this lonely tree
Has plenty of power to set men free?
Could it be this stark, rising pole
Could be that which makes sinners whole?

Oh, the cross, the cross, the glorious cross
For ages mankind has marveled at your meaning
For the plight of man is always lost
And needing someone to pay the cost

Why would not all run to your bloodstained base?
Why would anyone turn away their face?
The answer is hard yet true
That the stumbling block is really You

The tree where You sacrificed Your Son
Must be preached as the only one
The day You gave it all for me
On a hill crowned with an old rugged tree

Turn not your gaze, O sinner, from thee
The place of all redemption is Calvary
But many will turn away and disdain
The stumbling block that could end their pain

chapter three

THE REVELATION OF FAITH

I come to understand how I am joining Jesus in the fellowship of His suffering

"My heart was to be forever changed by the realization of His love for me. Nothing I would face would ever shake me from the foundation of this blessed truth."

The touch of God on my life had always seemed evident to those nearest to me. But after the healing power of God took hold of my life in Tulsa, His anointing and grace in my life accelerated.

The Spirit of God began to do great things in me. His leading and guiding started a firestorm of passion for Jesus that manifested itself in two different arenas. The first would signal a transition from my parents being the primary ones trusting God for my healing to my taking the dominant role in that pursuit. The other was an unexpected encounter with the Savior that would reveal to me His suffering and how it was far greater in measure and power than mine could ever be.

The Word of God

In the fall of 2001, I was exposed to the ministry of a traveling minister who challenged me to read the Word of God. He told me privately that he read through the entire Word of God once a month and had done so for years. Now, before this time, I had heard many exhortations to read my Bible, and none of them had had much of an effect on me. But somehow this man's enthusiasm for God's Word sparked a change inside me.

While before I had found a nice rhythm of devotion that was focused predominantly on praying and experiencing the presence of God, now I felt a voracious appetite for the Bread of Life. I saw the Word as the answer to all my problems. I remembered testimonies I'd heard in which others who were sick had undergone healing through the power of the Word. In particular, I recalled hearing Dodie Osteen, wife of the late John Osteen and mother of well-known televangelist Joel Osteen, tell how God had healed her terminal cancer through her daily declaring of forty verses from the Bible. I wanted that kind of experience! No longer did I just intellectually agree with the idea that the Word is the answer to all of life's issues; I had a self-perpetuating hunger for that Word.

How about you?

As you read this little book, I challenge you to press in to an appetite for the Word. Don't wait for some supernatural encounter, and certainly don't wait until it's too late for you to really get hold of God's Word on behalf of your situation. Do like Jesus, who was led by the Spirit into the wilderness and, having been there forty days, became hungry (Matthew 4:2). If you'll take a short break from food, you'll see how your appetites begin to change. Likewise, if you'll replace your regular diet of media with the presence of God in His Word, you will begin to crave the aroma of His fresh, living Bread as if it is all that matters. And it is!

During the last six months of 2001, I read through the Bible from cover to cover for the first time. What an exhilaration this was! My spirit man began to soar with strength and spiritual vigor. Yes, my body was still undergoing treatment and was weak at times, but my spirit man was beginning to take the lead.

Every believer should reach a point in their walk with Jesus where the resurrection life inside them takes over and they no longer are led by how they feel or what they want. This resurrection life will take you places you never would have thought to go and produce the precious fragrance that is life to those who seek it and a fearful smell of death to those despising it (2 Corinthians 2:15–16). My life was taking a radical turn. My ministry was being birthed, not by the experience of being raised in a minister's home, nor even by receiving a preaching gift, but by a real manifestation of God's Word. This life-giving Word was taking over my being, and as Jeremiah said, it was "like a fire in my bones!" (Jeremiah 20:9).

As the end of the year approached, I began to ask the Holy Spirit what He would direct me to do concerning the reading of the Word in 2002. (For me as a prophetic person, the end of the year is always a heightened time of listening for direction in the new year.) After some time in prayer, I was prompted to read the Bible through in one month. The challenge I had received to consume the Word was now moving to a new level, and I was ready for the challenge.

On January 1, 2002, I hit the ground running with my new assignment. All 1,189 glorious chapters of the Bible were going to be mine in the next thirty-one days. My plan was to divide the Word into sections and eat the elephant one bite at a time, so to speak. And that's what I did. Starting in Genesis, Psalms, Proverbs, Isaiah, and Matthew, I struck out on this great adventure.

If reading the Bible cover to cover in six months had been exhilarating, then words cannot express the spiritual fervor and excitement that flowed from consuming forty chapters of God's unchanging Word every day. The passion for God that followed reading His love letter to mankind is indescribable. My time pursuing Him in that month, coupled with our traditional time of twenty-one days of prayer and fasting here at Bethany, was a high point of spirituality in my life. The call of God was exploding, sensitivity to His voice was increasing, and my passion for the Lord Jesus Christ was intensifying so much so that I actually finished the mission of reading cover to cover in twenty-eight days—with three days to spare!

The faith of God was now working in me in a way that can come only from digesting the Word of God. Yes, one verse can shake the universe. But reading chapter after chapter was revolutionizing my heart. Fleshly pursuits and carnal behavior were being pressure-washed away by this mighty cleansing of God's Word. My system was being acclimated to heavenly manna and forever ruined to reliance on anything else.

That year would see me finish the Word five more times. The Holy Spirit was leading me deeper and deeper into the Scriptures with precious revelation that in the weeks, months, and years to come would feed not only me, but also a growing multitude of listeners. The Word was coming out of every pore of my being, and people were beginning to sense it. My opportunities to minister exploded along with my ability to communicate the Word. Some weeks I would give as many as fifteen messages. And that was subtracting three days a week for treatment! God was using all that I had experienced to form a foundation for this glorious ministry that was taking shape through His Word. My life was finally beginning to take on the form of the person God had called me to be.

After years of being cooped up in hospitals, tethered to treatments, and required to undergo surgery after surgery, I was now running with abandon toward the will of God for my life. But my newfound experience of God's Word was not all that He would use to transform me into a vessel to serve Him.

The Cross of Christ

Paul exclaims in Philippians 3:10, "I want to know Christ and experience the mighty power that raised him from the dead. I want to suffer with him, sharing in his death." The power of Christ's resurrection life had certainly taken over my mortal body, but now the Holy Spirit longed to introduce me to the fellowship of His suffering. He wanted me to see His glorious demise on the cross as if I had been there with John the Beloved and Mary, the mother of Jesus. He wanted me to gaze upon His humble death upon the cross and know that through all I had faced up till that point, I was "participating in the sufferings of Christ that continue for his body, the church" (Colossians 1:24), which began with what He faced for me on that terrible yet glorious day of Calvary's sacrifice.

Over the summer of 2002, as the Word continued to work mightily in me, the Holy Spirit wooed me in a way that I can only describe as a supernatural drawing to the cross of Jesus. Of course, I knew the cross as it pertained to my salvation, but as I would come to see, there was infinitely more to know than just coming to the cross for salvation. I would soon realize that the suffering of Christ on the cross was not only for the beginning of our journey with Him, but also for the entirety of our time on earth. We are to put aside our selfish ambition, shoulder our cross, and follow Him (see Matthew 16:24).

There is no way to truly follow the Master without carrying a cross on our shoulders.

This doesn't mean a weight of bondage, but a daily and sometime hourly reminder of what Christ suffered for us. His eternal sacrifice was the pinnacle of all time and would forever portray God's love for man and His promise of redemption by faith.

Surely, as a preacher of the gospel, and having been raised in the church my whole life, this simple principle would have been central to my spiritual walk, don't you think? Well, my friend, let me tell you that I was as oblivious to it as many in Christ are today.

One of the things about the cross that is so amazing to me is the unexplainable ability it has to offend. The late David Wilkerson said in his famous message on hell that many will see that rugged cross on the day of judgment and cry out in rage that this simple symbol was all that was needed for eternal life. The simplicity of the cross has been a stumbling block for mankind since Jesus hung there two thousand years ago. Man has done his best to make things difficult or mystical, but the fact remains that the simple work of Calvary is the only way to God. The offense of the cross doesn't stop with just those who are perishing, for in Christ there are still many areas of our selfish nature that must bow down and surrender to the wooden symbol of God's ultimate love. This was so for me in particular.

To me, hearing of the cross and feeling the prompting of the Holy Spirit to go deeper was a matter of offense. Surely I knew the meaning of Christ's death. Surely I, having by this point won many to the Lord myself through stirring altar calls and heart-rending messages, knew the power of the cross, if anyone did. Then the Holy Spirit spoke clearly to me one day and said, "If you had to preach an hour on the cross without any preparation or notes, could you do it?" And my immediate response was *no*.

This simple question revealed to me that I had little understanding or knowledge of the greatest act in human history. Our faith rests on Christ's work on the cross, and while I had experienced many deep revelations from Scripture and had heralded the principles and truths of God's Word from cover to cover, I was terribly deficient in the one message that counted most—the cross!

Once aware of this deficiency, I endeavored to press in to that fellowship of His suffering, to know Christ my Lord in the light of His grief and sorrow. He was acquainted with sorrows and pains like those that had plagued me for years. He is the Master of carrying our pain and misery. His love for us eclipses the greatest of human affection. This same love was now beginning to resonate in my life like a dusty bell that was now being rung again. It was if I had always known these things deep down in my spirit but had never seen them as clearly as if a "signboard of a picture of Christ dying on the cross" had been put before me, as Paul says in Galatians 3:1.

I remember going to the north sanctuary of our beloved church, falling on the altar before the Lord, and weeping in repentance of my pride and lack of gratefulness for His ultimate sacrifice. Over the next few months leading up to the end of 2002, the Lord brought me on a journey of His suffering like the Via

Dolorosa in Jerusalem. The glorious cross in all its simplicity and glory was descending on me. My ambition, pride, selfishness, and all other variables of the curse of sin were being crushed under the weight of Christ's cross. His revealed suffering was giving me life and liberty beyond imagination as my finite mind in some small way grasped what He had done for me.

After this time of revelation, my whole ministry took a turn toward the cross. Everywhere I went to minister, the Lord would have me preach the cross. Even when I wanted to move into something different, the Holy Spirit would insist that I preach the cross. First Corinthians 2:1–5 became the text I was known for because it was as if there were no other text in the Bible for me. To my amazement, freedom and joy followed the preaching of this gospel everywhere I went. Many would weep and wail in the aftermath of my preaching on the cross and would then be filled with the joy of the apostles when the Lord appeared to them alive. Without deep repentance at the cross, there cannot be lasting joy at the resurrection.

My life was to be forever marked by the fellowship of Christ's suffering. My heart was to be forever changed by the realization of His love for me. Nothing I would face would ever shake me from the foundation of this blessed truth.

If you're sitting today in a place of self-pity or find yourself absorbed in a life of selfish pursuits, I challenge you to look up at the rugged cross and see the bleeding Messiah hanging there for you. One glimpse of His love, one moment of His suffering, and you will be shaken from selfish pursuits. All things not pertaining to His eternal purposes will begin to die, and only that which is of His divine will and nature will remain. That cross will shake everything that can be shaken until all that remains is that which is unshakable (Hebrews 12:26–27)!

With the Word of saturating my mind and the passion for Christ's cross burning in my heart, I was ready for the work God was soon to reveal.

The Valley
July 31, 2012

POEM OF REFLECTION

Whatever goes up must come down
Whenever there's high, there must be low
For every smile, there's always a frown
For every good, the bad takes a blow

The moments on high keep life worth living
But reality of pursuit can be unforgiving
To find the valley more than not
Will force tissue to continually blot

While mountaintop will bring exhilaration
The valley will force deep reflection
When things go right, why stop to pause?
But things gone wrong make easy the flaws

The mountain, excitement it brings
In valley, you find life's subtle springs
The art of refreshing one's soul
With no one around to hold and cajole

Oh, valley, how we easily disdain
The hurt, disappointment, and pain
Don't stop your work now or refrain
The bitter food you serve will forever train

My soul wishes to pass over with haste
To stay atop the world with the sun on my face
But God in His wisdom has put you in place
That wisdom and faith would be said of my case

Oh, valley, don't come so often to me
When I see you my tendency flee
Even out the high place your job to be
Done all too well with your sweet misery

chapter four

THE CALL OF FAITH

In the midst of my own health trouble, God lays a burden for the next generation on my heart

"You cannot wallow in self-pity or the misery of your present circumstance but must seek the Lord and find His place of fulfillment for you."

Many times the Lord will equip you in the comfort of a position or place and then make that same place steadily uncomfortable in order to move you into the mission for which you were equipped. It's much like what happens to an eaglet that is enveloped in the warm, inviting nest until it is ready to fly. Its parents then begin to place glass in the same nest they had once prepared for comfort. That's just what happened to me.

As the fall breezes of 2002 began to blow, the revelations I had received on the Word of God and Christ's sacrifice on the cross began to churn a divine discontent within me. Two events of significance would change my heart and direction for life. They would lead to my discovering—to my great surprise—the kind of ministry God had for me.

A Word to Stay

The first life-changing event for me in those days was an encounter with my good friend Dr. Rodney Howard-Browne. I had traveled to

Tyler, Texas, to be with him and R. W. Schambach for a special time of impartation, and one night after the meeting, I found myself sitting at dinner with Pastor Rodney. We had sweet fellowship, and he was asking me of my life and plans. I'll never forget the wisdom he shared with me.

His words to me from decades of experience in traveling with the gospel were these: "You can travel around and bless a lot of people, but you should stay with your father and build something lasting."

Those words resonated in my spirit. I had been seriously contemplating going on the road full-time to declare my newfound revelations to the national body of Christ and accepting some of the many invitations I was receiving. My one great hesitation in the midst of all this was my continued battle with kidney failure. The shackles of the dialysis machine were still holding me to a clinic three times a week and made travel difficult for me. Now this man of God had given me a word of wisdom to stay put and build something lasting.

How would that work? What did God have in mind? I wasn't sure. But I recognized the voice of the Lord speaking through this mighty vessel.

A Word of Confirmation

A second event would confirm this radical new direction in my life. It came from none other than my direct authority: my natural and spiritual father, Larry Stockstill.

I rejoice in the father I was given in this earthly journey. He has been there for me through every deep valley and celebrated with me on the mountain peaks. His steady hand has stilled my raging storms, and next to the Lord Jesus, he has been my rock more than any other.

Over Thanksgiving week in 2002, I began to share with my father the discomfort I was feeling in my ministry. "What do you think the Lord would have me do?" I asked. I continued on, listing all the excuses of why it was so difficult to travel with my health, but how it seemed inevitable that the message the Lord had given me must get out to the rest of the world.

As I stood there in my parents' kitchen, my father said, "Why don't you think about taking over the youth?" He was talking about me becoming pastor over the youth ministry at Bethany World Prayer Center.

"The youth?" I responded. "No way! I don't want to take over the youth."

I had never liked youth ministry and the babysitting feel that seemed to pervade most youth ministries. To me, youth ministry had always just been something for those who were not ready for big-folks ministry. Plus, how would a young person ever receive the great treasures of revelation that God had entrusted to me?

All these issues were racing through my mind, yet there was also a supernatural peace in my heart and a real sense of direction in all of this. Although I was aggravated at first, I now look back in thanksgiving for the sense I had to discern the voice of God speaking directly to me by my authority.

Isn't it interesting that God's voice sounded exactly like Eli's to Samuel (1 Samuel 3)? Isn't it easier for the Lord to direct you through someone more seasoned and mature than you? Why look high and low for direction when many times you can receive it so simply by the voice of your authority? Remember this: If you heed direction, then you won't need much correction!

The Lord was doing something with me that would change the course of my entire life, and if I had followed my own reasoning, I would have missed this opportunity by a country mile.

As the final weeks of the year passed, I would hear a louder and louder witness in my spirit that I was truly supposed to move into the leadership role of our youth ministry. Yes, I had preached to our youth from time to time over a period of several years, but now the Lord was calling me to put my entire energy and ministry focus on what I would later find to be a generation in desperate need of deliverance. Moses didn't see going back to Egypt as a glamorous job that he had always dreamed of, and I didn't see moving into youth ministry as something to be greatly desired—but that was all about to change.

Setting Sail by the Wind of the Spirit

After a season of transition, my hands firmly gripped the position of youth pastor in March 2003. The Lord started visiting me in the way of great compassion and vision for a generation. This passion would go far beyond corralling a handful of kids in the back room on Wednesday night and would become a raging fire for heaven to be revealed. Every meeting, whether leadership or prayer, seemed to lead inevitably to me weeping and many times wailing with the yoke of burden that was meant for my shoulders. It was only later that I could look back and see that it was the cross I was to bear for Christ in the form of reaching a new generation with the gospel of Jesus and the revelation of His delivering power found only in the cross.

For three months, through the middle of that year, I was under a divine visitation of God's Spirit that would not relent until every fiber of my being was consumed with a heart for this generation. The Lord spoke to me in that season and impressed upon me Jonah 4:11, where God says, "Nineveh has more than 120,000 people living in spiritual darkness…. Shouldn't I feel sorry for such a great city?" As I researched the current demographics of Baton Rouge and the surrounding area, I found the exact same number of teenagers living around me. The Lord said to me, "You must reach them all with the message of the cross so that no one from here can say they never heard about My great love for them."

Wow! This mandate began to burn within me. Far from my preconceived notion of baby-sitting in the back room, my vision and passion had now become a regional assignment to bring the message of the cross to every young person. The burden that fell on me those three months would light a fire that burns brighter today than ever.

Though from time to time I was still going through the routine procedures and surgeries associated with being a dialysis patient, my heart was ablaze with a fresh sense of purpose. And this has shown me something I want to share with you: When you are in the midst of an ongoing battle and pain seems to be never ending, you *must* find the purpose for your life. You cannot wallow in self-pity or the misery of your present circumstance but must seek the Lord and find His place of fulfillment for you. If you're still alive, then there is purpose for you! If God were truly done with you, then you would be in eternity right now. No matter how the winds may rage against you, lift up a sail of obedience and allow the Lord to carry you places never imagined by your carnal mind.

By His supernatural guidance, my spiritual sail was up, and I was being led into greater and greater levels of His call on my life. He knew the plans He had for me (Jeremiah 29:11). He led me step by step, and He will lead you with His gentle hand to the pastures of greatest fulfillment *if* you'll just trust in Him and the call He's placed on your life.

Armed with a fresh burden and call to a generation, I began to build the ministry as the Lord directed. Not being much of an evangelist, I was going to need a divine strategy in order to meet the mandate given to me by the Lord. This is where the next great revelation of my life would come, along with a piece of self-awareness that would clue me in to the ministry the Lord would have for me for the remainder of my life.

My New Math: From Addition to Multiplication

By the coordination of the Holy Spirit, I met and began a relationship with a man of God named Cesar Fajardo from Bogotá, Colombia. This man had built a youth ministry of over seventy-five thousand. Yes, *seventy-five thousand*! And it was all built upon the model of disciples going out and making disciples. To me, it sounded like a real-life manifestation of

Matthew 28:19, where Jesus declares, "Go and make disciples of all the nations." This man of God inspired me and imparted to me the necessity of raising up disciples who could do the work of the ministry with the same passion and spirit that I possessed.

In this simple truth came the divine strategy that I had sought. The answer was not for me to get the biggest crowd possible in the traditional sense of services and programs; it was to pour my life into willing vessels who would go out and do the same (2 Timothy 2:1–2). This effect would move past the limitations of addition in the church and release an anointing of multiplication that would be far more potent.

It was time to multiply! I really had no grasp on how to carry out this new strategy, but I had the hunger and humility to seek it out and work it out.

As 2004 progressed, this newfound revelation of discipleship consumed my energies. Finding young men and women who were yielded and ready to run with this newfound vision became my obsession. There weren't many at first—but then, Jesus took only twelve! I ended up with seven—four men and three young ladies. (I mentored the young ladies in how to disciple, but not in their characters or personal lives; that was a job delegated to a seasoned woman in our ministry.) These seven leaders would become the pillars and model for what would soon become hundreds of young people who were hungry for more than just attendance and longing for true discipleship. This discipleship was not a class of information, but a whole ideology of impartation. My soul was thrilled as I saw the Lord using me to impart what He had given me to faithful men and women and they in turn imparting to others. My struggle was now becoming my strength. My hard-fought revelations were becoming useful for the kingdom.

When we face the adversities of life and the fiery trials of our faith, it is imperative that we keep pressing toward the call that God has for us. When you are sitting inactive and reflecting only on where you are or what has happened in the past, your faith lies dormant, and fear and doubt rise to the top. But when you are determined to sink your teeth into God's call on your life, even if it seems small and insignificant at first, the faith of God that was deposited in your spirit like substance in a seed will begin to activate and produce results. Faith is centered upon action, and not just any action, but doing the will of the Father for your life.

My struggle for health was still raging on, but my call was motivating me to move forward day by day. As treatment after treatment would come and go, night after night of sleeplessness and pain, week after week of facing medical hardship, my call to young people drove me on. My faith in a mighty God kept me focused. My strength in the Word kept me fresh with belief for the impossible, even while facing hardship at every turn.

Meanwhile, at the same time God was blessing my work in ministry, He began to bless me in my personal life as well. It turns out, I wouldn't be fulfilling His call on my life all on my own for long.

Flipped
February 22, 2012

What do you do when up is down?
What happens when a smile is really a frown?
What do you do when life deals a crooked hand?
Like a delightful plate that is terribly bland

What's the use of a world gone astray?
Where day is night and night is day
Where sleep replaces the time of play
When moments of thought have nothing to say

What happens to a world that is always flipped?
When full life has seemed to be constantly gypped
Where the hand of sickness holds tight in its grip
And life seems to pass in a grinding drip

What can be done to right this sure wrong?
To make things go back where they belong
Until then I'll be consoled with a song
Yearning with all my soul for the dawn

chapter five

THE LIFE OF FAITH

G od sends me a loving partner for my
work and trials

*"Faith puts your spirit first. Faith denies the
reasoning of your mind, the negative tendency
of emotion, and the stubbornness of your will
to accomplish the impossible."*

As so many amazing things were happening in the ministry side of things, I felt a deep longing in my heart for companionship—not the surface kind that we find with casual friends, but a deep, meaningful relationship with a woman of God that would last for a lifetime. I had always looked forward to marriage, and yet in the midst of my struggles and revelations, I had never found "the one." Oh, how my soul longed for this great joy! And yet my battle with kidney failure ground on, and love seemed nowhere to be found.

For a stretch of about two years, I didn't even find someone to be curious about. Knowing that God was doing big things in my heart and life brought some comfort to me, but at the end of the day, we all want a special relationship with another human being that brings fulfillment.

My pitiful romantic life was soon to change!

A Gift from Heaven

In August 2003, we held our fortieth anniversary at Bethany World Prayer Center. My grandfather—Brother Roy, as he is affectionately known—started our church in his living room in August 1963. This little Holy Ghost church would rise to be an influence around the world in decades to come, and now we had guests from all over celebrating with us what God had done from that small beginning.

During that weekend, I was placed on the platform to play my violin for some of the special music we were doing. (Violin was a huge part of my early life. Beginning lessons at age five, I would see my skills grow until I earned first place in a national competition at sixteen and then received a full scholarship to college based on my musical ability.) From the platform, I could see everything going on in the congregation. As the final service was ending with a climax of Communion, I looked down and saw a beautiful woman walking in line across the front of the church to receive her

Communion elements. As it happened, when she approached the table, they temporarily ran out of the wafers, and she was stuck standing there for a lengthy amount of time, thus allowing me to get a good look at her. Well, she might as well have had a neon arrow over her head as I wondered who this tall, beautiful woman was!

After the service, my family went out to eat at one of our favorite local spots. I turned to my brother Jonathan, who had been leading worship, and said, "Did you see that girl who was stuck up front during Communion?"

He quickly replied, "Yeah, I did. That was Amy Hart. Do you remember her?"

I did remember her but had not seen her in five or six years—and boy, were things different!

Not five minutes after our conversation, I looked out the window. Guess who I saw walking toward the door of the restaurant? Yes, it was Amy, the beautiful woman from church. Something was going on!

She entered the restaurant and ended up coming over to our table to say hello. Taken aback, I couldn't muster much more than a grunt for a reply. But I was struck by her from that moment forward.

My life would never be the same after that hot, sunny day. The Lord had brought along someone who could not only share my life, but who also possessed the strength to manage the heavy weight of dealing with my health. After a few months of friendship, Amy and I began to date in December 2003.

One night, as we traveled to New Orleans to celebrate Amy's birthday—April 1, 2004—a deep sense of destiny fell on us, and we knew something special was happening. That night we confessed our love for each other and decided to be married. My heart was thrilled!

The Lord had brought an amazing woman into my life, and the fact that I had fought alone for years made it that much sweeter. Life is many times about contrast. If you don't know bad, then you can't appreciate good. If you've never had lack, then you find it hard to appreciate prosperity. In my case, for nine years hardship and pain had been my constant companion, and now this gift from heaven was to be the joy of my heart.

Taking the Sunshine with the Rain

Amy and I made plans to be married in October in the Virgin Islands—and the race to the wedding was on! Those days passed swiftly. Yet I thoroughly enjoyed the engagement period, wedding, and newlywed days, thankful to God every minute for His goodness to me and my marvelous new bride.

Let me make an observation here: When you are fighting a serious adversary of illness or heartache, you must learn to appreciate and celebrate the things that give you joy. Many who are in such a situation tend to lump everything together into the bad and not see the rays of sunshine that do break through the clouds of hardship. And indeed many people face hardships I couldn't imagine. But I know that if you will learn to distinguish between the good and the bad in your life, it will keep your hope alive.

The attitude of faith is to continue to believe for good even in the midst of real adversity. This hope will be attractive. It will cause others to be inspired by your hardship instead of turned off by your attitude. I've made many mistakes along the way in dealing with chronic illness, but I've found that I can be either an inspiration or a burden to others. I want with all my heart to inspire people through my pain and not demoralize them through my complaining. Won't you have the same goal?

When you expect good things, you will find them. When you expect negative things, they will overrun you!

In Amy, I had a very good thing indeed. But the companionship I had always dreamed of was put to the test almost immediately after we were married. By December 2004, some ugly issues with my health were back on the scene, and from then until the end of March 2005, we were forced to live in West Palm Beach, Florida, under the care of my beloved physician, Dr. Chauncey Crandall. Living in his garden home, Amy and I were thrust into some intense medical situations that tested us both to the limit. For her, it was a crash course in Joel and the seasons of tremendous hardship that would plague our lives in the years to come.

This time was also an opportunity for our faith to grow together. Learning to believe God together is something that is easier said than done! Feeling almost abandoned to ourselves in a beautiful but lonely place, we learned to share the Word of God and worship the Lord together whether in the hospital or just hanging out. Even though this time was difficult, a bond developed between us that was uncommon for a young couple. The fires of affliction melded us, and we left that season with an amazing closeness and a surety of faith that God was going to use us together for His glory.

Meanwhile, the precious youth ministry the Lord had given me (now called 220 from Galatians 2:20) was faltering under the lack of leadership resulting from my extended health battle in Florida. As I received reports of things happening back home, my heart was heavy with the question we've all asked so many times: *why?* Over and over I prayed, "Lord, why would You allow this battle to keep me away from the burden You gave me for the youth of Baton Rouge?" This question and the intense battle all around me drove me to much prayer. Night and day, I was seeking the Lord for His will and plan.

One day in March, several weeks before we were to leave Florida, the Lord visited me with a divine strategy for 220. He showed me how to consolidate our ministry under the most seasoned leaders and regain a mighty momentum for the fall and the beginning of school. At that time, we had a little less than one thousand kids being discipled, and it seemed as if we would never break that barrier. My faith knew that we could, but my mind didn't know how. Boy, does that sound familiar! After receiving the plan of action from the Lord, Amy and I returned to Baton Rouge and went to work implementing the strategy given from the Lord.

Faith in Operation

Beginning in April 2005, I laid my hand to the plow and didn't look up until fall. I was graced with a season of reprieve in my health—as suddenly as things had gone from bad to worse, they turned around and I was able to do the work of several men. Even having only four days a week (with treatment taking up three days), I was still able to accomplish amazing things. The grace that was working through me was similar to that on Paul in Ephesus (Acts 19), and I felt a momentum of growth coming that drove me day after day to the task of reaching every teenager in our city. The plan given to me by the Lord led up to a final leadership retreat before school started in the fall of 2005, and on that retreat the glory of God was poured out. We laid hands on one hundred of our greatest leaders and commissioned them to go forth and harvest a great crop of souls for the kingdom of God.

As if on cue, the next week Hurricane Katrina hit the Gulf Coast, and our plans were thrown into disarray. Our hard work seemed to be for nothing. But my faith was not going to give up! I had been through too much and had worked too hard to have some hurricane stop what the Lord was going to do. God told Noah that the one thing he could count on after the flood was seedtime and harvest (Genesis 8:22). I had planted the seeds, and now it was time for the harvest.

One thing you can be sure of is that if you plant nothing, then you will reap nothing. If you allow your situation to demoralize you and keep you from doing anything, then you will be sure to reap a big fat nothing in the future. No matter how hard your road may be, the principle of seedtime and harvest will always remain.

I referred earlier to Mrs. Dodie Osteen and her victory over terminal cancer. She decided to plant the seeds of healing in her situation by going to the cancer wards and praying for the sick. There she was, barely able to walk, and yet she was out ministering to others. She received a harvest of healing herself. No one said it would be easy. It may be much harder for you. But you have to trust God and put some seed in the ground!

I had worked four months with diligence and expectancy, and now I knew that something was going to happen. And boy, it did!

After six weeks of confusion and chaos left in the wake of Katrina, we finally reassembled our team of leaders and implemented the plan for mass harvest. Immediately we broke the one thousand mark, and by the first week of November, we were reaching more than two thousand kids a week with the message of the cross and providing the discipleship needed to help them grow into mature Christians.

I had worked two and a half years for one thousand, and God had multiplied us to two thousand in less than six weeks! My heart was full of excitement. My faith was soaring. Jesus had once again multiplied the loaves and fishes to feed the thousands. Once again He had handed out His precious Word to disciples, and they in turn brought it to the masses. My eyes had now seen something that the enemy would never be able to retract. My faith had worked, and kingdom expansion had happened. It was like the Wright brothers flying for the first time![1]

When you see faith in operation on any level, it will thrill your soul. Your mind, will, and emotions will feel exhilarated as never before when the spirit man comes first. Faith puts your spirit first. Faith denies the reasoning of your mind, the negative tendency of emotion, and the stubbornness of your will to accomplish the impossible. God is looking for this faith in you.

God is pleased only when He sees this faith at work. He is not looking for emotional highs or brilliant ideas from us. No, He is looking for us to believe Him even in the midst of great struggle.

The disciples had a legitimate reason for being afraid of the storm, yet Jesus rebuked them because they failed to believe He was

---

[1] To learn more about the 220 youth ministry, see 220power.com.

more than able to handle the situation (Mark 4:40). So I challenge you today to allow the faith of God to operate in your life. No matter how small or great the step, you need to take it! I realize that you may not know what to do. But if that is so, ask the Holy Spirit to show you what seeds you can plant to bring forth a harvest of joy in your life. Then do it.

Be warned: The answer you get when you pray for guidance may not be what you want to hear or be something you're comfortable with. In the days of Elisha, the great Syrian general Naaman didn't like his seed of instruction one bit. He didn't want to humble himself by dipping in the muddy Jordan. It took some of his officers to bring the proper perspective. After all, a dip in some muddy water is nothing compared to the awful fate of leprosy (see 2 Kings 5:1–14).

What is the Lord asking you to do that will release what you've been asking for? Is it a financial seed? Is it an act of obedience that you've been ignoring? Is it to reach out to someone you have not forgiven and be reconciled? Nothing in this world should keep you from your miracle.

Allow the Holy Spirit to lead you today. For those who are led by the Spirit *are* the sons of God (Romans 8:14), and what good thing has He withheld from those who love Him? *Nothing!*

4 Years ...
February 14, 2012

In Memory of Amy

4 years today you were laid to rest
At the time it seemed like a dream
The kind that are definitely not the best
The kind that really make you scream

4 years ago we said our final good-bye
With tears and sadness overwhelming our souls
There in the grave did you lie
With fleshly remnant of love already grown cold

4 years have passed so fast in many ways
With life moving on like a river downstream
So many things you wish you could say
But the fact that you're gone seems always to bring

4 years have eked by ever so slow
As marker by marker ignores your glow
We pledge in our hearts to never forget
No matter how many years your memory may sit

4 years may just be the start
Of all we have felt since we had to part
Only God can know the length till we meet
By the pearly gate on heaven's gold street

chapter six

THE TEST OF FAITH

I give my wife back to God, learning to trust in Him even in the worst of circumstances

"When hardship or tragedy overtakes you in any way, don't run from the Lord in hurt and disappointment; run to the Lord Jesus and appreciate His love."

I'll never forget the exact doctor's-office chair I was sitting in when I heard the word "cancer" spoken about my beloved for the first time.

For several months, Amy had been bothered with a knot on her neck, so finally we visited our local ENT for a biopsy. Weeks later, in May 2007, we went back for the follow-up visit, and as usual we were laughing and talking, even holding hands. The love that we shared was deep, and the joy we found in each other's presence was not that of your ordinary couple.

As the doctor came in and began to talk about the situation, an ominous feeling began washing over me. When the "C bomb" came out, I went into full-fledged shock. This was certainly a mistake! This could not be! The thing given me by God that I treasured the most—my wonderful wife—was being put in a sentence with the word we dread the most for ourselves or anyone we know, much less love. *Cancer*. Amy would later be fully diagnosed with non-Hodgkin's lymphoma.

Walking out of the doors of that medical facility with Amy, I was totally stunned. I heard myself reassuring my wife that this was a ridiculous stunt of the enemy. But inside I was reeling.

Shortly after this visit, a test would confirm the initial diagnosis, and the doctor would prescribe chemotherapy. Our life together would never be the same.

Heading Home

Already by this point in my life, I had faced so many surgeries and procedures that my body was littered with various scars and reminders of the brutal battles I'd fought against sickness. But this was my beautiful wife, and she had no such scars. Her skin had never been cut by the surgeon's knife; her veins had never been punctured with needles; her life had never taken any such turn of tragedy as this. Within a month of the diagnosis, though, all that would change. The first step was to put in a port for the chemo needles. It seemed that every little step taken after that was an excruciating reminder of the reality of our situation.

At this point, I made a mistake that, as I look back on it, grows clearer and clearer to me. Instead of founding my faith on the Word of God and His promise of divine health and abundant life, I kept telling myself that surely God would not allow anything more to come my way in the form of hardship. And surely He would know that my beloved's dying would be much more than I could handle. Didn't He promise in 1 Corinthians 10:13 that we would never have more than we could handle? Well, temptation, not sorrow, is the subject of that verse—and God has a lot more faith in what I can handle than I do!

So here Amy and I were, with me facing all my usual health struggles just as before and with her now battling cancer. It was a crazy season. Both our mothers stepped onto the scene with the tenacity only mothers can have. One would cart me to treatment, and the other would cart Amy to chemo. Both of us were being stuck by needles in ports, and both of us were extremely weak afterward.

For several months starting in June 2007, the cancer in Amy's body responded to the treatment, and the size of the deadly lymphoma was shrinking. We were becoming optimistic. We had learned that the cure rate for non-Hodgkin's lymphoma—if treated early—was 95 percent. And so far the doctor's reports in Amy's case were positive. So there was a time when I thought that although we were going through a horrific trial, we would make it out on the other side just fine.

That lasted till October, when things mysteriously took a turn for the worse. The cancer stopped responding to treatment and began to grow again.

This was all compounded by the fact that with the increased doses of chemo being given to try to reverse the cancer, Amy's beautiful long hair was falling out and came down to a few strands. The day she finally let me shave her head was a day of such sorrow and pain for us both that it cannot be told in words. I wept and she wept as I finished off the last strands of her once thick and glorious covering. Things were starting to look grim. Though she wore wigs that fooled most people, at home the complete absence of her hair was a constant reminder of what was ever seeming to be her death sentence.

We were then sent to M. D. Anderson Cancer Center in Houston to seek out specialized treatment options, and the trekking back and forth from Baton Rouge to Houston began. Sadly, I was unable to be with Amy on many of these trips because of my own incessant need for kidney treatment. But in any case, her condition did not improve.

After all had been tried and had failed at M. D. Anderson, we were told about a place in Mexico just across the border from San Diego where a godly doctor was seeing amazing results from natural therapy. We arranged for Amy to go out and see if this last attempt at health would work. The plan was for her to be there for three weeks at the end of December and the beginning of January, and I would go out in the middle week to see her.

My visit was dominated by struggling with treatments and long border lines going back and forth. But this time was precious to us, as it was the last time we would be together with Amy able to talk normally. On the day I was to return to Baton Rouge, I lay next to her and kissed her on her perfect head while we shared a few precious hours unhindered by sickness or pain.

Six weeks later, on February 11, 2008, my wife and dearest friend went to heaven.

To this day, the details that preceded this home-going are too painful for me to recount. Perhaps one day I can tell the story more fully. At this point, even in the midst of my unimaginable loss, I welcomed the victory of eternity and Amy's release from her suffering and pain. The irony of it all, of course, was that people had felt sorry for Amy in marrying me with the type of health situation I was in, and now here I was, at twenty-eight years old, burying my first wife!

But let me back up for just a moment to tell you about the night Amy died. Everything had gone wrong in her condition, and we had returned to the local hospital in Baton Rouge. The doctors performed emergency surgery on Amy. As I entered her darkened room in surgical ICU, with machines galore and the sound of life support whooshing, Amy's form lay quiet and unmoving in the bed. Then the Holy Spirit spoke to me as clearly as I've ever heard His gentle voice. He quickened Genesis 24:60 in my spirit and said, "She will be known as the mother of millions." The Holy Spirit was speaking to me of a legacy that would be hers from the portals of eternity. At that moment, I knew Amy was in God's hands.

Tears began to stream down my face as I reckoned with the fact that she was gone. But I also felt a strange sense of peace. I had not been told by any doctor or social worker that it was over. No, the precious Holy Spirit, my Comforter, had come to let me know what was now to be a lifelong reality of sorrow and yet peace. His presence descended on me like that of the dove that came to rest on Jesus in the waters of baptism.

I'm so thankful for the Lord's presence at all times, but in that moment His presence was especially precious to me. He truly is a God who will never leave you or forsake you. He *is* touched with the feelings of our infirmities (Hebrews 4:15). I was experiencing Him and His vast love in a way that I had never experienced it before. I was enveloped in His hand for that seemingly impossible moment, and this would be the taste of comfort to come.

Three days later, on Valentine's Day 2008, we laid my beloved wife to rest. Her spirit was gone, and all that was left was a shell, but we mourned over her and buried her with great dignity. She wore a blouse I had bought for her on our honeymoon in Saint Thomas. Even in death, her beauty was unaffected. Thousands flocked to what would be one of the largest funerals I've ever seen. The love and goodwill were overwhelming. Friends from all over America flew in to mourn with me and celebrate the life that was Amy's. She was one of a kind, and none could ever replace her. Her legacy would go on with the many she had touched. Her life would never be forgotten and her ways always looked on with joy.[2]

This was the darkest night of my life. To God be all glory that I made it through!

How Faith Survives

Following all these happenings, life gradually, fitfully resumed its normal course for me.

From the night Amy passed away, I never spent a night alone for the next year. My amazing family came together and stood in my support. (I am the oldest of six kids, with four brothers and one sister ranging fourteen years apart.) The support started with my father, who—as I stated earlier—has always been my rock. He stayed at my house with me that week and gave me a shoulder to cry on. There would be times of reflection and other times of

---

[2] To watch Amy's home-going service, go to joelstockstill.com.

pure grief. Crying and speaking of Amy's dear life made the pain ease. My younger brothers James and Jason would take turns staying with me and keeping me entertained. My brother Jared would later move in with me for several months. Jonathan, who married Amy's younger sister Angie three months after my marriage, made an apartment in his upstairs for me to come and stay three days a week. Everyone pulled together and helped me to walk out of a dungeon of grief. Moment by moment and day by day, I moved one small step further to recovery in my heart.

If you have lost a loved one in any manner, be comforted today by the Holy Spirit sent from above. Jesus said that He would not leave us as orphans, but that He would send the promise of the Father in way of the Holy Spirit (John 14:16–18). I know what it is like to not want to read your Bible. I know what it is like to have people offer "comfort" that just makes things worse. My experience in those times was something that put me in a certain "club" of those who have lost loved ones so precious and dear. There were days of such sorrow that I couldn't face the world and then days when God's unending joy would be amazingly tangible. My heart was thrilled at the thought of dear Amy in heaven, but it was also filled with hurt at the loss of her companionship.

One day shortly after the funeral, her parents came to what had been our house and loaded up all of her stuff. Yeah, it was just stuff, but it was *her* stuff. This brought me a serious feeling of closure. It was tough but helped me to see that gone were her things and gone was her laugh. Gone was our time and gone were our dreams.

My faith had been rocked. My heart was aching and my mind was reeling. Everything I had stood for and taught for years was being tested. My faith for healing in my body was shaken. Would I encounter the same fate as had befallen my dear wife? Would such great sorrow be my constant lot? How could I have been through so much in my life and then something unexpected come along and trump it all with sickening effectiveness? The questions began

to come like a flood. My mind was unrelent-
ing in its barrage of logic that demanded some
answer of fact. But the truth was, there was no
answer that could soothe my anguished soul.
I could only rest in the presence of the Savior
who died for me. I made His presence my ref-
uge, and when the questions and doubts would
try to sink my boat of faith, I would wake up
the Master and rest in His arms.

When bad things happen in your life, the
questions will come. And they will drive you
crazy. They may even try to drive you away
from the Lord Jesus. But if you have trust in
Him, it will drive you to Him for the glorious
embrace of His love.

It's okay to have questions like I did as
long as you end up with the answer I found.
My answer was always Jesus. My mind didn't
like it, but my heart was satisfied every time I
embraced the Master from Galilee. The love He
poured out when He hung on the cross would
be far more than anything I could ever find
on this earth. The love that drove Him to Calvary would be more passionate and alive than

I could have ever dreamed. And yes, I had seen His suffering on the cross and been transfixed by His death before, but now my fellowship with Him in His sweet suffering was deeper and richer than ever before. The highs and lows came in their demanding way, but the presence of Jesus always calmed the storm.

Your faith may have never been tested this way, but the lesson of His presence is nevertheless the same. When hardship or tragedy overtakes you in any way, don't run *from* the Lord in hurt and disappointment; run *to* the Lord Jesus and appreciate His love. Turn on worship music that magnifies the Lord. Lift your hands in worship to Jesus, whether you feel like it or not. Get into a place of fellowship with other believers where you are safe from the dangers of isolation. Don't allow your feelings to run wild and wreck what remains on the shores of doubt.

My soul needed healing but never lost sight of the Master who could right any wrong and heal any pain. Jesus, my Lord, was more real to me than ever before.

When walking through the valley of the shadow of death, allow the Great Shepherd to comfort you (Psalm 23:4–5). Let Him anoint you with His anointing oil and cause your cup to run over. Let Him prepare a table for you even in the presence of your enemies. Let Him bring comfort to you even in the midst of seeming defeat.

In His time and in His way, He'll turn things around for you. That's just what happened to me.

Reborn
June 2, 2010

It started what seems so long ago
A day to never be forgotten
Since then so very much has happened
Day after day, blow after blow

My ship was wrecked on shores of grief
Robbed by sickness, both mine and hers
I've longed many nights for relief
But only sorrow did I find

And then a shining star I saw
A glimmer of hope to be
Could this ease my unending sorrow?
Could my grief really come to an end?

With grace and love you rescued me
Your laugh and cheer found their mark
To be the one to change my life
Would be the course of God's plan for you

I kneel before you this starlit night
Filled with joy untold
To ask you for once and all time
To be my darling wife

chapter seven

THE
ENDURANCE
OF FAITH

God restores the sparkle to my eye:
a new beginning

*"Today is the day to arise from the
hopelessness and misery of yesterday and set
your eyes on the one who gave it all for us."*

Grief is long. It arises and recedes and returns again like waves on the seashore. In the midst of my ongoing grief during the months after I lost Amy, many Scripture passages became important to me, none more so than the heart cry of Psalm 13.

> O LORD, how long will you forget me?
>   Forever?
> How long will you look the other way?
> How long must I struggle with anguish
>   in my soul, with sorrow in my heart
>   every day?
> How long will my enemy have the up-
>   per hand?
> Turn and answer me, O LORD my God!
> Restore the sparkle to my eyes, or I
>   will die.
> Don't let my enemies gloat, saying,
>   "We have defeated him!"
> Don't let them rejoice at my downfall.
> But I trust in your unfailing love.
> I will rejoice because you have rescued
>   me.

> I will sing to the LORD because he is
> good to me.

"Restore the sparkle to my eyes, or I will die." There couldn't have been a more appropriate verse to articulate the "anguish in my soul" in the wake of losing my dear Amy. There seemed to be "sorrow in my heart every day" as I tried to move forward toward life and love again. But move forward I did.

Meeting My "Rebekah"

I made a promise in my heart to take one year to grieve for Amy's loss and to honor her memory. And I did that. But I have to admit that I (since I was still a man, after all) started noticing certain young ladies from time to time. None caught my eye like the young and vivacious Amie Hope. Amie had been a member of my youth ministry for years, but because of the size of the ministry, we had never met.

You might be asking yourself right now, *What's up with Joel and that name Amy or Amie?*

Well, I'm not sure. But it seems like the Lord has sent women with that name into my life on several occasions to bless me greatly. It's not just Amy Hart and Amie Hope. There's also my long-time assistant and good friend, Mrs. Amy Roberie (who after my wife's passing stepped in to lead and disciple the young ladies of 220). So it seems as if the Lord has given me some sort of drawing to the Amy/Amie contingency of females.

Anyway, from time to time I greeted Amie in a casual manner and began to think of her at times. But that's as far as it went during my avowed year of grieving. I really did desire to honor Amy in the best way I could by reflecting on her memory for a solid year before pursuing other interests. Still, you must remember that here I was, a twenty-nine-year-old man with a long history of chronic illness and a deceased bride. There was no way that I was going to remain single for a long amount of time!

Back to the sparkle.

My thirtieth birthday fell on March 12, 2009. Over a year had passed quietly but surely since the day I'd lost Amy. My brother Jonathan and his wife, Angie (who was the younger sister of Amy, remember?), decided it was time for me to spread my wings and begin the process of seeking new love and companionship. (This was all probably heightened by the fact that they knew I couldn't live in their nursery-to-be for much longer!) They informed me that a birthday dinner was to be held in my honor at a prestigious restaurant in New Orleans, and I was expected to attend and bring someone—someone female. Well, in my mind, there was only one person that I wanted to spend that type of an evening with.

I acquired Amie's phone number and called her out of the blue. She was surprised. Yet she would display in this situation an example of the tremendous poise that would guide her through many touchy and difficult scenarios over the time of our courtship.

She agreed to my invitation to accompany me that evening, and our friendship began awkwardly at first because of my being in San Antonio for front-row seats at a Lakers game and her riding down for the hour-long trek to New Orleans with a car full of people she didn't really know. (Brave soul!) I arrived late, which I despise doing, and she was already seated all by her lovely self waiting on me. This would be a prophetic picture of what was to come.

The Lord had kept this beautiful lady hidden in His hand for such a time as this. Though six and a half years younger than me, she was the one the Lord had for me to spend the rest of my life with. On that night in New Orleans, it took little time for us to enter into conversation as if we were in our own little bubble. And when that night was over, we began a friendship. After an extended time of hanging out and getting to know each other in group settings, it became evident to me that this was the girl for me.

Nothing confirmed it like the October night of worship when I was asked to play my violin. It just so happened that as I looked down the neck of my violin, I saw the lovely Ms. Hope sitting about eight rows back. We had not talked much lately, and she was busy finishing her interior design degree from LSU. But now, as I looked down on her worshiping the Lord, He said to my heart, "She is the mother of your children." (Isn't it interesting that both times when the Lord revealed my bride, it was while I was playing the violin?) The message couldn't have been clearer. This young lady was the one to bring the sparkle back! Oh, how my soul rejoiced!

Many years before, in 2001, the Lord had spoken a word to me one day as I meditated before Him. This word came from the end of Genesis 24 (the same passage in which I would later hear Him speak on the night when Amy passed on). The Lord said, "Rebekah will come into your tent and comfort you in the wake of your loss." This meant absolutely nothing to me at the time. And later, when I was married to Amy, I thought back to this revelation and told myself, *Well, I must have just missed it.* Ha! Little did I know that years later, as I meditated in the field as an older Isaac, God would send me a young lady across the desert of my loneliness to comfort my heart and bring fresh love (see Genesis 24:63, 67).

Some Things Change, Some Things Don't

In December 2009, Amie and I expressed our romantic interest in each other, and we began to date after that. The sparks began to fly. It wasn't long before things became serious.

Being the prophetic person I am, I wanted to be like Gideon and put a fleece before the Lord for His confirmation of our future (Judges 6:33–40). This test came in the way of an invitation for Amie to join me in Seattle for a ministry engagement and to celebrate my birthday once again—this time just the two of us. She flew to Seattle and met me for a most memorable night when we got a flat tire and all sorts of things went wrong. The one thing that went right was our dinner at the top of the Space Needle. What we ate that night was forgettable, but the feeling we shared was not. Our hearts seemed to soar with love for each other, and a sense of peace that we were to be mates for life descended upon both of us. This was the sign from heaven I was looking for!

By June 2010, we were engaged, and on September 4, we were gloriously married at my beloved north campus of Bethany World Prayer Center, where I had been pastoring for four years. It was the biggest wedding I've ever seen, with over fifteen hundred people in attendance. So many people who loved me were there in support of this grand day just as they had been there to grieve with me in that same building for my grand loss. There was tremendous joy in the atmosphere, and as my beautiful bride walked down the aisle, I surprised her with a violin rendition of "Come in My Courts," a worship song I had written about the Bride and the Bridegroom. What a special moment! What a day of victory! From the depths of anguish and grief to the heights of love and joy, this story was one of great pain and great triumph. For a brief moment in time, it seemed as if my life was finally starting to make sense. Would this be the end of all my struggles?

I wish I could tell you that from that moment everything turned around and all sickness and disease lay behind me. But that would not be the next step of this up-and-down story of mine. The form of battle that followed was unlike anything I had met before, as multiple small issues began to plague my health. I entered into a season of procedure after procedure. From four attempts at repairing one of the main valves of my heart, to constant maintenance of my dialysis access, and on and on, the "small foxes" came to spoil the vine (Song of Solomon 2:15).

A week or so before Amy passed away, I had asked my parents how it was that I got picked for reliving the Job character. Who signed me up to always be the picture of the suffering servant of the Lord? Now facing many physical battles once again, and all this time enduring treatment after treatment three times a week, I returned to this question of identity with the Lord. I could have said with the psalmist, "How long will You forget me, Lord? Forever?" To this present day, the battle rages for my health, as years of wear and tear have taken their toll, and the health and vitality of youth seem to have abandoned me.

In the midst of continued resistance and struggle to move forward, the Lord has given me grace to continue in the call that was irreversibly placed on my life. My dear wife Amie and I have our hands full with the oversight of 220 as well as our church internship and newly formed Bible college. I also travel throughout the United States preaching the gospel and teaching leaders as the Lord gives me strength and health.

I'm thankful to God that I have Amie by my side now as I go through all the challenges this life has to offer. Not only does she bring me joy, but she is also a steadfast support, and with her I can face whatever lies ahead.

Endurance through Christ

It is here that we come to the climax of what I want to say in this little book.

What do you do when all you've hoped for has not yet come? What can you do when you've sung every song, quoted every verse, listened to every sermon, been prayed for by anybody and everyone? The simple answer to that question is *endure!*

James said in the opening of his letter, "Dear brothers and sisters, when troubles come your way, consider it an opportunity for great joy. For you know that when your faith is tested, your endurance has a chance to grow. So let it grow, for when your endurance is fully developed, you will be perfect and complete, needing nothing" (James 1:2–4). This is the best passage I could think of to describe the work the Lord has done and continues to do in me. In fact, if I had to pick just one word to describe my walk of faith and the journey that I have lived, it would be James's key word "endurance."

This aspect of faith is so precious to the Lord. Oh, how we love the stories of faith listed in Hebrews 11, stories such as those of David slaying the giant and Daniel shutting the mouths of lions! But what about the others who never saw the fulfillment of the promise of God while living on this earth? For example, what about Isaiah, who is alluded to as one of the "others" of Hebrews 11, who was sawn in half (verse 37)? This is not to discourage you or anyone else from believing that your time or miracle will come. But in the end, what if it doesn't? Is your servitude to the Lamb of God based on your getting what you feel is rightfully yours? Yes, Scripture makes promises, and we stand on those promises with tenacity and courage, but does God have to make something happen in order for your loyalty to be unquestioned?

Out of all the great things I've learned on this journey—the revelations, visions, and miracles—the greatest thing I've learned is to *trust* the Lord no matter what and continue to live a life of thanksgiving and worship despite present circumstances. There have been unbelievable highs of God's presence and anointing on my life, along with many devastating lows, but in the midst of it all has been an almighty

God who sent His only begotten Son to be brutally sacrificed on a tree so that my sin and shame would be paid for and my life could be abundant and eternal.

This perspective can seem easy and obvious when times are good, but it's hard and distant when trouble comes knocking. To repeat, David said:

> I trust in your unfailing love.
> I will rejoice because you have rescued
>   me.
> I will sing to the Lord because he is
>   good to me. (Psalm 13:5–6)

The goodness of the Lord that David talks about is not contingent upon how we are feeling today. No! We should rejoice every day that our names are written in the Lamb's Book of Life.

The Lord *has* rescued me! Though the battle of kidney failure and all its wicked cohorts may still rage against me, and though the death of my precious first wife may taunt me, I will *rejoice* in the Lord my God and not allow feelings or circumstances to rob me of the proper perspective.

This is the endurance we have been called to. This is the pathway to God's greatest riches in glory found only through Christ Jesus. This is the sweet fellowship of His suffering that bears the precious fruit of obedience. For even Jesus Himself "learned obedience from the things he suffered" (Hebrews 5:8). If our Lord and Savior had to walk the road of suffering to find sweet surrender to our heavenly Father, then what must we think when trials come our way but that opportunity for greater fellowship with the Lord has come knocking? Never celebrate bad things in your life, but don't despise the moments of God's testing and the trial of your faith, for they *will* cause your faith to come out as pure gold (1 Peter 1:7).

I exhort you today to the great labor of endurance—not just weathering the storm, but believing in a miracle-working God who has brought you this far and will be faithful to finish His grand work in your life. My struggle with hardship has not left me hopeless, but rather hopeful to see the goodness of the Lord in the land of the living (Psalm 27:13).

The three young Hebrew men said to Nebuchadnezzar, "The God whom we serve is able to save us. He will rescue us from your power, Your Majesty. But *even if he doesn't*, we want to make it clear to you, Your Majesty, that we will never serve your gods" (Daniel 3:17–18, emphasis added). These young men were right. They were faithful even to the point of death, and God *did* rescue them.

So He has done for me.

So He will do for you.

What's Yet to Come

As this book comes to a close, my prayer is that you will not just have found my story interesting, but that you will catch the heart of my words. To some, this book may seem like a common-enough story of loss and hardship. But if you look at its spiritual meaning on the inside, it is really a triumphant story of faith and endurance—not because there's anything so special about me, but because there's every-thing special about my gracious Savior! And regardless of what you have been through so far in your own life, this story of triumphant faith and endurance is the kind of story you can have for your own.

Today is the day to arise from the hope-lessness and misery of yesterday and set your eyes on the one who gave it all for us. I leave you with this passage from Hebrews 13 that sums up the message of my little story for you:

> Jesus suffered and died outside the city gates to make his people holy by means of his own blood. So let us go out to him, outside the camp, and bear the disgrace he bore. For this world is not our permanent home; we are looking forward to a home yet to come. (Hebrews 13:12–14)

Be blessed, my friend. And stay tuned for more!

conclusion

I pray that this booklet has caused your faith to soar to new heights. I wrote it to encourage and strengthen the faith of all who believe as well as to stir the hope of those who have given up.

There is a God who loves you. His Son, Jesus, loves you with an unquenchable and unfathomable love. That love drove Him to set aside His glory in heaven and be born here on earth to give Himself as a sacrifice for the sin debt you could never pay. This precious sacrifice satisfied the wrath of God toward sinful man (you and me) and made a way for you to enter God's presence with right standing and approach Him whenever you desire without fear.

If you don't know the Lord Jesus Christ, I urge you today to accept Him into your life. He is the author and finisher of this great faith I've written about in this booklet. Without Him, all is lost and nothing is promised of tomorrow but darkness and judgment. Join me in this marvelous walk of faith and watch how God's glorious presence fills your life. Will things be perfect? No! But as David declares to God in Psalm 84:10, "A single day in your courts is better than a thousand anywhere else!"

If you connected with me through my story,
you can continue to follow my journey at:

www.joelstockstill.com